Extreme Quilt

MW01131763

Extreme Quilters, in an informal association of fiber artists founded in 1997 in Southern California. We create, share, critique and apply surface design techniques to cloth. Many group members have exhibited work in prestigious juried exhibitions nationally and internationally, and have works placed in private collections.

This is our 14th annual show at the Thousand Oaks Community Gallery. We are so pleased to exhibit in person, and share this year's work with you.

- Lynn Jurss, founding member & catalog editor

Cover: art quilt by Sue Rasmussen
Postcard design by Loris Bogue & Rodi Ludlum
Catalog design by Lynn Jurss
Photography by Lynn Jurss or the artist

Copyright © 2023 by the artists
ISBN: 9798860939516

First edition September 2023

Extreme Quilters 2023

Standing: (L to R): Sue Rasmussen, Pamela Christner, Lynn Ben-Chetrit, Linda Stone, Lynne Willcox, Loris Bogue, Rodi Ludlum, Linda W. Fisher, Joan DeYoung, Sarah Hart, Christina Rocha, Janice Lynn Jurss, Janice Prezzano

Seated: Celeste Covas, Diana Shore, Sandra Sigal, Guila Greer, Leone Keegan

Not pictured: Eileen Alber, Margarete Heinisch, Sandy Harper, and Lisa Miller

2023 Exhibitors

Adages and Idioms Challenge:

 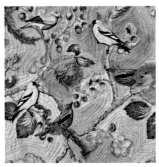  

Choose a favorite adage or idiom and bring it to life.

   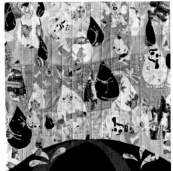

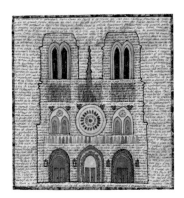  

Lynn Ben Chetrit

Agoura Hills, CA

Black Horse
10W x 15 H

Lynn Ben Chetrit
Agoura Hills, CA

White Horse
14 W x 23 H

Lynn Ben Chetrit
Agoura Hills, CA

Zebras
19 W x 14 H

Lynn Ben Chetrit
Agoura Hills, CA

Adages and Idioms Challenge
Through Thick and Thin
18 W x 17 H

Loris Bogue
Simi Valley, CA

Murder of Crows 2
26 W x 28 H

Loris Bogue

Simi Valley, CA

Eddy
35 W x 35 H

Loris Bogue
Simi Valley, CA

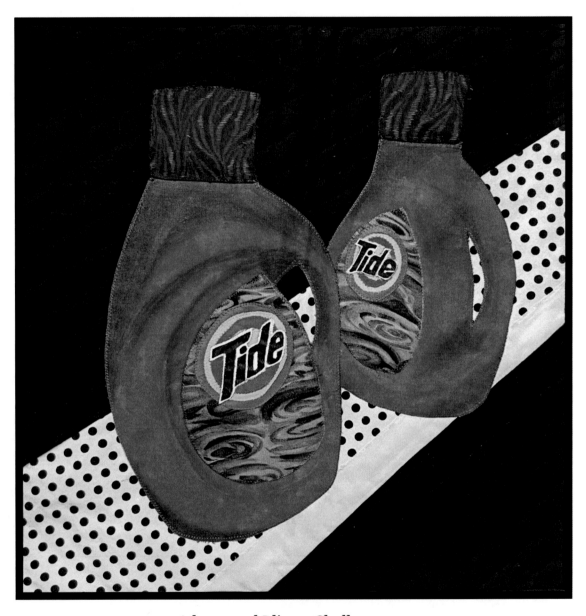

Adages and Idioms Challenge
The Tide Has Turned
18 W x 18 H

Pamela Christner

Bishop, CA

The Hawk
19.5 W x 18 H

Pamela Christner

Bishop, CA

Collage II
11 W x 19.5 H

Pamela Christner
Bishop, CA

Adages and Idioms Challenge
Red Shy in the Morning
17 W x 14 H

Celeste Covas
Bell Canyon, CA

Blue Vase Still Life
16 W x 20 H

A simple still life with raw edge appliqué on hand dyed and stamped fabric. Embroidery is added to give the geometric pattern in the background more texture.

Celeste Covas
Bell Canyon, CA

Recycled materials and appliqué on a hand dyed and printed background. Translucent teabags and transparent voile embellished with inks and give this

Children with Birds
13 W x 19.5 H

Celeste Covas

Bell Canyon, CA

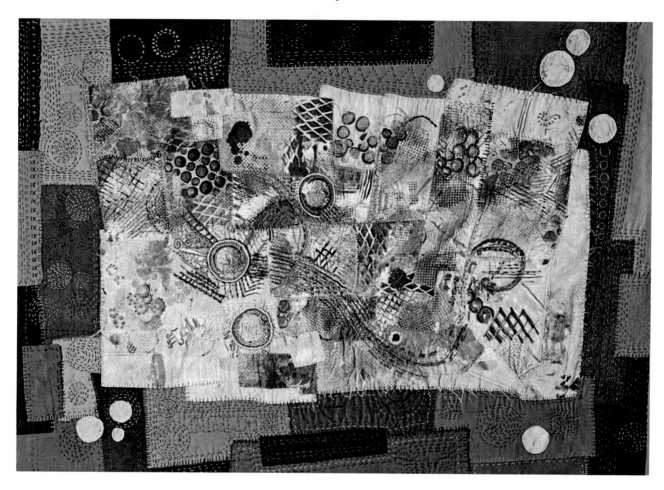

Yellow and Purple
Composition
38 W x x26H

Whole cloth multi media design using marking tools which include
stamping, with dyes, inks and paint. Entire cloth is deconstructed
and reassembled with embroidery to create an entirely new

Celeste Covas

Bell Canyon, CA

Imagine the delight of opening the window and a wild bird gently lands on your outstretched palm. This quilt collage consists of hand rendered images and raw edge appliqué with couched hand made and dyed string and profuse hand embroidery to give it texture.

Adages and Idioms Challenge
A Bird in the Hand
18 W x 17 H

Joan DeYoung
Thousand Oaks, CA

Mayan Temple
32 5 W x 25.5 H

My visit to Teotihuacan, Mexico and climbing the Sun and Moon Pyramids, as well as visiting Chichen Itza's unique Mayan Temple which has 91 steps on each side plus the top step which equals 365 were my inspiration for this quilt.

Joan DeYoung
Thousand Oaks, CA

The floating flowers are caught between the background fabric and an overlay of sheer fabric which changed the colors. if you look at the back of the quilt you will see the original fabric. Choosing a sheer that gave the fabric a watery effect determined the of design this quilt.

Floating Flowers
15.5 W x 20 H

Joan DeYoung
Thousand Oaks, CA

Adages and Idioms Challenge
Birds of a Feather
18 W x 18 H

This collaged piece was made using home Dec fabric which I painted and appliquéd birds and free form embroidered feathers.

Joan DeYoung
Thousand Oaks, CA

The background tie fabric has an overlay of sequenced mesh. The circles are stitched on using a couching technique, the mirrored children are running around reflecting the colors of the quilt.

Adages and Idioms Challenge
Going Around in Circles
18 W x 18 H

Linda W. Fisher

Santa Paula, CA

Windows of Gold
29 W x 35 H

The day after Christmas 2022 I walked through the front doors of what would become my very own home. I knew someday I would try to make an art quilt of those front doors. While looking for an idea for this year's quilt I remembered a story by Helen Steiner Rice about Windows of Gold, and that became my inspiration. The quilting design matches the backsplash in my kitchen.

Guila Greer
Tarzana, CA

Bees and other pollinators are responsible for supplying 90% of the world's nutritional needs. In the meantime, bees are being threatened by pesticides and other toxins. It's a huge problem but even you and I can help combat the loss of our bee population. Whenever possible, be sure to include pollinator plants in your gardens. Then, get ready to welcome the bees into your garden.

The Bee Comes for Lunch
30 W x 30 H

Spring Has Sprung
11 W x 14 H

Do you remember the catchy ditty - Spring has sprung, the grass has riz. I wonder where the birdie is. The bird is on the wing. How absurd! The wing is on the bird! I remember it and this is what I was inspired to create while that ditty went around and around in my head.

Guila Greer

Tarzana, CA

Do you remember the catchy ditty - Spring has sprung, the grass has riz. I wonder where the birdie is. The bird is on the wing. How absurd! The wing is on the bird. I remember it and this is what I was inspired to create while that ditty went around and around in my head.

The Grass has Riz
12 W x 16 H

Guila Greer
Tarzana, CA

Beach Buddies
20 W x 16.5 H

A special memory captured - our 2 year old granddaughter strolling on the beach with her beloved Poppy John. In addition to this very special relationship, the photo and subsequent quilt document forever this 2 year old's lively taste in clothes and an enduring love of bright colors.

Guila Greer
Tarzana, CA

Since 1959, residents of Windsor Ontario Canada and Detroit Michigan USA have gathered together annually to celebrate freedom. The celebration occurs between July 1, Canada Day and July 4, USA Independence Day, and culminates with a festive fireworks display on the river.

2 Cities, 2 Countries, 1 Border - Celebrating 2 Centuries of Peace
18 W x 24 H

Guila Greer

Tarzana, CA

Adages and Idioms Challenge
Loose Lips Sinks Ships
18 W x 18 H

Be careful with your words. Lives and Empires have been lost by a careless word whispered into the wrong ear.

Sarah Hart

Thousand Oaks, CA

Solarpunk is an optimistic, hopeful punk genre that imagines a future where technology provides solutions to climate change in local sustainable communities. This piece imagines little eco-friendly, solar-powered cloud-seeding machines making water precipitation for people and farms. Solarpunk art is represented by sunny colors, art nouveau style and includes traditional gears or old fashioned power sources with sci-fi elements.

Solar Punk -
Water Harvesting
35 W x 57 H

Sarah Hart

Thousand Oaks, CA

Still Life with Milk
Glass Vase
12 W x 16 H

Fabric and acrylic splash painted canvas cloth, cut and resewn in the quilting style.

Sarah Hart
Thousand Oaks, CA

Fruit of the Vine
12.5 W x37 H

Loved the sunny leaves and vines in my Solarpunk piece and wanted to continue the art nouveau style and create a piece celebrating wine and grape vines. I had not planned for the tiny zigzag sewing around each little grape, but happy with the final result.

Sarah Hart

Thousand Oaks, CA

Kyoto Spring
18 W x24 H

Kyoto is famous for its gardens and classical Buddhist temples and Shinto shrines. Kyoto is a very traditional city and depicts the charm of rural Japan.

34

Sarah Hart

Thousand Oaks, CA

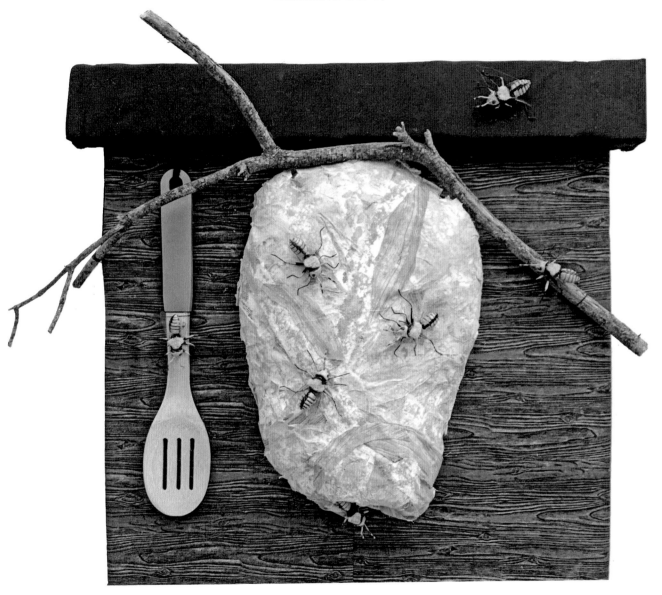

Adages and Idioms Challenge
Don't Stir Up the Hornet's Nest
18 W x 18 H

Margarete Heinisch
West Hills, CA

Playing with Nature
12 W x 16 H

In a workshop I played with different materials, Angelina fibers, paint, and interfacing to create this nature scene.

Margarete Heinisch

West Hills, CA

Adages and Idioms Challenge
Once in a Blue Moon
18 W x 17.5 H

Longing
11.25 W x 13.25 H

Based on a photo I took of house across the street from my yoga class. The expressions on the cat and dog priceless. Commercial cottons, organza, paint.

Lynn Jurss
Thousand Oaks, CA

I captured color and light during wildflower season on a bluff overlooking the Pacific Ocean. Vintage silk, polyester, and wool neck ties, cotton and linen.

View from Point Dume
46.5 W x 54.75 H

Lynn Jurss
Thousand Oaks, CA

Shine on You Crazy
Diamond
51.75 W x 67.5 H

Constructed from the ugliest striped polyester and silk neckties from the 1960's and 1970's in my collection. It is an homage to a favorite band of my youth, Pink Floyd. Polyester, silk, cotton.

Lynn Jurss
Thousand Oaks, CA

Malpais, "badland," portrays the colors and light at that Malpais National Monument near Grants, New Mexico. Vintage silk, polyester and wool neckties, wool, and silk.

Malpais
34.5 W x 42.75 H

Lynn Jurss
Thousand Oaks, CA

Milagros
44.25 W x 56.5 H

Inspired by several trips to New Mexico. I've kept a small collection of milagros, small tin charms, that are used to pray for intercession or relief. They adorn church chapels in Santa Fe.   Cotton, fabric paint, trapunto.

Lynn Jurss
Thousand Oaks, CA

New Mexico is dotted with markers and tributes to people who have died on the roadway. I created vignettes representing the wide range of these tributes. Commercial cotton, silk ribbon and cotton embroidery, appliqués, found items, paint.

Descansos - Highway Martyrs
30.75 W x 40.75 H

Adages and Idioms Challenge
Dumpster Fire
12.5 W x 15 H

Dumpster Fire was word of the year in 2016, and has been applicable for something every year since. Need I say more? Cotton, paint, photos printed on fabric, watercolor pencil.

Lynn Jurss
Thousand Oaks, CA

The clown car coup gang. How can half the country be so duped by their lies? Cotton, photos printed on fabric.

Adages and Idioms Challenge
Elect a Clown, Expect a Circus
12 W x 16 H

Leone Marotta Keegan

Bell Canyon, CA

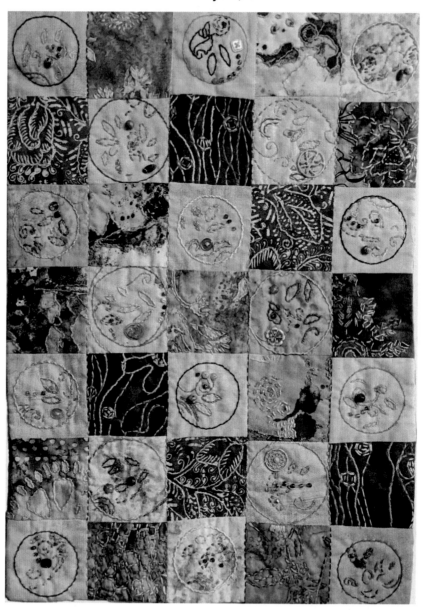

Adventures in Sevens
15 W x 21 H

Hundreds of scraps became a 35 piece art quilt. Each square is embellished with embroidery, beads, and buttons

Leone Marotta Keegan

Bell Canyon, CA

Discovered at a thrift store, the handkerchief guided the path of the fabric applied. Embroidery with beads

Antique Handkerchief
& Me
16 W x 20 H

Leone Marotta Keegan
Bell Canyon, CA

Oil in Threads
10 W x 20 H

An impressionist Masterpiece interpreted in thread. Changed glass bowl into woven form, oil-rendered white fabric returned to its cloth form, enhanced apples and pears with colored thread.

Leone Marotta Keegan

Bell Canyon, CA

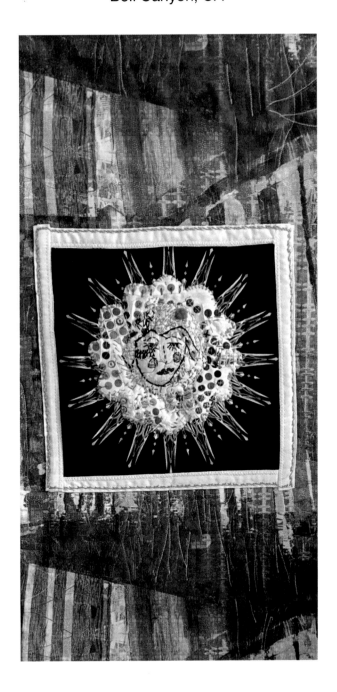

Salute
14.5 W x 28.5 H

Inspired by attending my niece's passing, ending her decade-long battle with breast cancer. A privilege. Embroidered.

Leone Marotta Keegan

Bell Canyon, CA

Window Scene
18.5 W x 24.5 H

Twelve individual displays of the divine feminine and nature. Fabric images created with appliqué, embroidery, and beading.

Scrap Dolls

Dolls constructed from scraps and given individual personas. Traits by hand-sewn appliqué and embroidered threads for hair.

Leone Marotta Keegan

Bell Canyon, CA

Adages and Idioms Challenge
Light at the End of the Tunnel
17 W x 17.5 H

Memories of car rides as a child on vacation on the East Coast. Entered darkness and exited into magnificent foliage. Appliqué with hand embroidery.

Rodi Ludlum

Agoura Hills, CA

A friend gave me the stuffing from a crib bumper, which I rolled and used for the long tail on this dragon. The fearsome spikes are leftover pieces from making fabric bowls.

Baby Bumper
15.5 ft long

Rodi Ludlum

Agoura Hills, CA

Santa Cruz Boardwalk
23 W x 20.H

Hand embroidery passed the time on many long train journeys.

Rodi Ludlum

Agoura Hills, CA

Hand embroidery passed the time on many
long train journeys.

Space Junk
23 W x 20 H

Rodi Ludlum
Agoura Hills, CA

Adages and Idioms Challenge
Draw Fire
18 W x 18 H

I combined my nephew's dragon drawing with a photo of Seattle to make a scene of graffiti artists using using fire as their paint...or "drawing fire". Of course they are wearing fire fighting gear so they won't suffer too much for their art. .

Janice Prezzano
Westlake Village, CA

In viewing this piece, you may feel a sense of quiet and peace which mimics my feelings while stitching. Hand sewn.

Tranquility
17 W x 11.5 H

Janice Prezzano
Westlake Village, CA

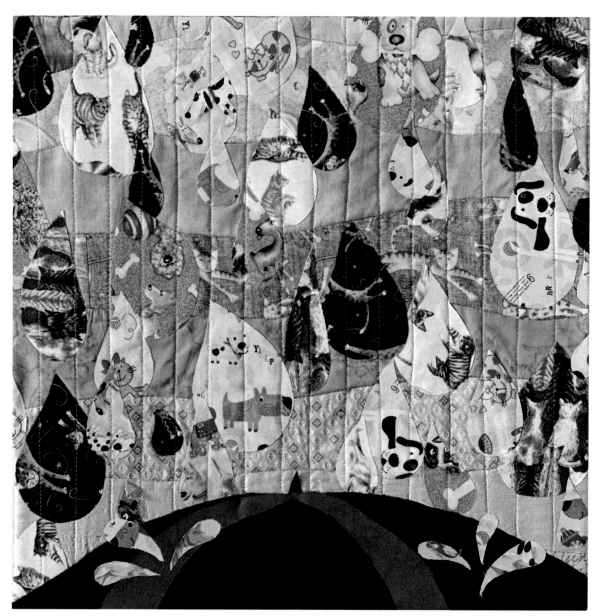

Adages and Idioms Challenge
It's Raining Cats and Dogs
18 W x 18 H

Curved piecing, fusing, machine stitching.

Sue Rasmussen

Simi Valley, CA

Original design by Vicki Garnas
Machine appliquéd and quilted.

Goblin and Gourds
45 W x 49 H

Sue Rasmussen
Simi Valley, CA

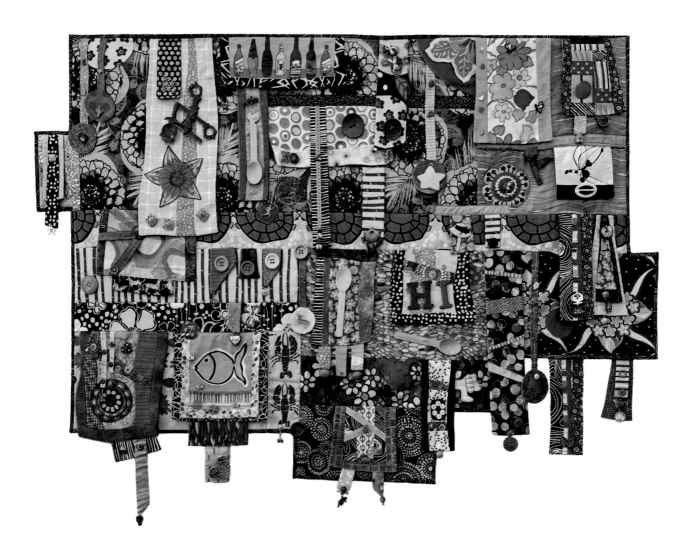

Honi Honu (Kissing Turtles)
49 W x 38 H

Inspired by Dianne Hire quilts from Pinterest 2nd attempt at this type of multi layered quilt, embellished with anything I could find.

Sue Rasmussen

Simi Valley, CA

Inspired by Dianne Hire quilts from Pinterest
I stumbled and fumbled my way along creating this 1st quilt, since I
had no idea where to start. Embellished with everything I could find.

Mardi Gras1
41 W x 30 H

Sue Rasmussen
Simi Valley, CA

Pomegranates
19.5 W x 19 H

Begun in a Sue Benner workshop. Photo found on free clip art. Fused with Pellon 805, mono-printed, painted, machine quilted.

Sue Rasmussen

Simi Valley, CA

Made for the SAQA auction-$ from sale proceeds will be donated
to SAQA. Présage has a sense of foreboding, a harbinger of the
unknown.

Présage
12 W x 12 H

Sue Rasmussen

Simi Valley, CA

Red Birch Trees in Lourmarin
24 W x 28 H

Original photo taken in France.
Fused with Pellon 805 and machine quilted.

Sue Rasmussen

Simi Valley, CA

Outlined image from free clip art, enlarged, drawn on painted fabric, painted with Alcohol Art Pens, fused, painted, and 1000 words hand written in French about the history, fire, architecture and importance of Notre Dame de Paris.

Adages and Idioms Challenge
A Picture Paints a 1000 Words
Notre Dame de Paris
17.5 W x 18.5 H

Christina Rocha

Newbury Park, CA

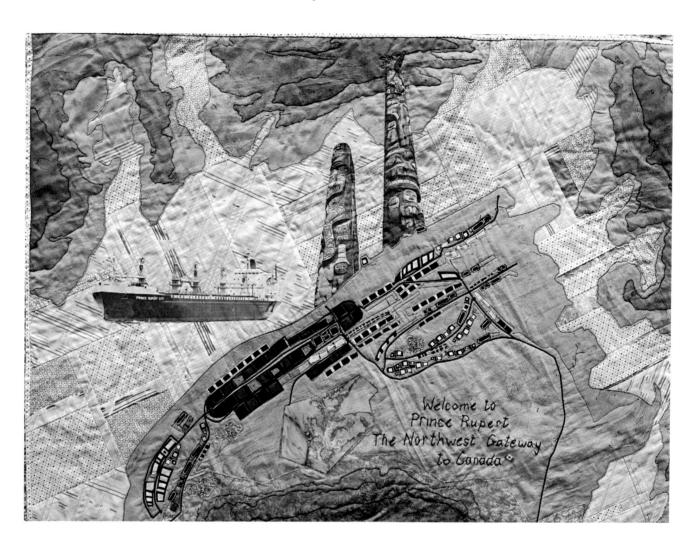

Welcome to
Prince Rupert
The Northwest Gateway
to Canada

Prince
Rupert, BC
36 W x 26.5 H

My hometown. Considered the halibut capital of the world when the Canadian Fish & Cold Storage Plant opened in 1912. The 1980's brought the collapse of many Canadian fisheries and the new slogan for Prince Rupert became the "City of Rainbows".True to its name, this coastal city in the northern shores of BC is the rainiest city in all of North America.

Christina Rocha
Newbury Park, CA

In 2019, record fires engulfed much of the Brazilian amazon rainforest. The holes in this piece represent the loss of forest due to human desire to make way for agriculture, livestock, logging and mining.

Brazilian Flames
46 W x 46 H

Christina Rocha
Newbury Park, CA

Near Side of the Moon
34 W x 23 H

An exploration of shapes, couching yarns and delving into my button stash to add dimension.

Christina Rocha

Newbury Park, CA

An exploration of shapes, couching yarns and delving into my button stash to add dimension.

Dark Side of the Moon
34 W x 23 H

Christina Rocha
Newbury Park, CA

Dad's Gallbladder Surgery
11.5 round

My father had surgery years ago to remove his gallbladder. I started a Surgical Technology program last year and was engrossed in anatomy and other science classes where I learnt about the procedure to remove the gallbladder, a cholecystectomy. I just graduated in August and started my new career in the operating room at Los Robles Medical Center recently.
Embroidery incorporating beads, yarns and felted "gallstones."

Christina Rocha

Newbury Park, CA

Adages and Idioms Challenge
"If you can't get rid of the skeletons in your closet,
you'd best teach them to dance"
George Bernard Shaw
18.5 W x 13 H

Coincidence of
Opposites
44 W x 40 H

Brushed stainless steel shadows and dance poses inspired the design while strips of my figure drawing paintings provided the background. The piece incubated under my father-in-law's grand piano and soaked up his classical chords of harmony. Harmony requires two voices that synergize as one. The opposing curves are the flip side of each other. The truth of anything is contained within the tension of two opposites. No thing is one thing.

Diana Shore
Hidden Hills, CA

In gratitude and caution we avoid the "evil eye."

Survivor
8 W x 8.L x 20 H

Diana Shore
Hidden Hills, CA

Adages and Idioms Challenge
Challenge 1
16 W x 18H

This diptych repeats the Jewish adage from Pirket Avot, "You are not obligated to complete the task; neither are you at liberty to desist from it entirely. Someday, it will be complete as will I.

Diana Shore
Hidden Hills, CA

Adages and Idioms Challenge
Challenge 2
16 W x 18 H

Sandra Sigal

Encino, CA

Collaboration
28 W x 28 H

My daughter has been using this shape in some of her current artwork. I borrow it to make this quilt. When it was completed it looked to me like talking heads. I didn't want to put eyes or mouths on the shapes, but wanted to leave the interpretation to the viewer. Maybe you see something different in it. Machine appliquéd and quilted.

Sandra Sigal

Encino, CA

Sue gave me a bag of scraps. It is always fun and a challenge for me to see if I can put scraps together in a way that is artful. The dandelion is made from hand dyed silk. The quilt is machine pieced, appliquéd and quilted

Dandelion
31 W x 36 H

Sandra Sigal
Encino, CA

Joy is a Valid Compass
19 W x 24 H

Hand-dyed the quilt's background. Then, whimsy got a grip on me. One of those truly joyful days. Got to dive into my scrap stash (love that). Snuck in some scraps from a sample pack from a Spoonflower workshop. I did the machine appliqué and quilting to finish it off.

Sandra Sigal
Encino, CA

Marti, my friend, spilled the beans on this trick during a quilt meetup. You whip up your usual log cabin blocks, then slice then into quarters – vertical and horizontal. After that, you shuffle the quarters around from different blocks and put them back together. It's a blast, not too tough, and the outcome is thrilling

Log Cabin Variation
38 W x 38 H

79

Sandra Sigal
Encino, CA

Portuguese Tiles
28 W x 34 H

I took a trip to Lisbon last spring. One of the highlights of the trip was the tile museum. So many fun designs to use for quilting. These are replications of two of the tile designs I saw in the museum. Lucky for me, my friend Marti gave me some blue and white fabric at just the right time. It is machine pieced, appliquéd and quilted

Sandra Sigal

Encino, CA

Sue and I had a lively playdate dyeing the quilt's background by hand. When Celeste took a look and it brought back memories of a lakeside spot where she'd summered with her kin – loons, wildflowers, berry picking. Appliqué and a dash of beading brought those scenes to life on this quilt. And, to top it all off, I added machine quilting to amplify the effect.

Sheepscot Lake
19 W x 34 H

Sandra Sigal
Encino, CA

Warm Next to Cool
41 W x 41 H

I got a couple of bags of scraps from my friend Rodi. Rodi's all about bright, bold fabric colors. Thought I'd give the warm and cool colors side-by-side a try like my art teacher, John Paul Thorton, suggested for maximum drama. While I was quilting away, I took it to a quilt meeting. My good friends there thought throwing some circles in would amp up the whole thing!! And it worked.

Sue's got a thing for passing on her UFOs to me. This quilt began with one of those. It had a sky vibe. I hand painted the birds with Liquitex fabric paint. And well, I just couldn't help but add some extra flair. The rest of the stuff on the quilt is machine appliqué and quilting

Who's Watching Who?
28 W x 18 H

Sandra Sigal
Encino, CA

Woven Silk
29 W x 36 H

The woven part of this quilt is hand dyed silk. It is dyed with alcohol inks. I used commercial batik fabric for the background. The challenge was to find background fabrics that would contrast with the weaving. Machine appliquéd and quilted.

Sandra Sigal

Encino, CA

He did it!!! The haystack is made with fabric "crumbs" and a bit of felt. Machine appliquéd and quilted.

Adages and Idioms Challenge
The Needle in the Haystack has been Found!!
15 W x 19 H

Sandra Sigal
Encino, CA

Adages and Idioms Challenge
Keep Your Eyes on the Ball
16 W x 19 H

I heard this expression so many times
when I was raising my four children. I
hand-dyed the background fabric.
Machine pieced, quilted and appliquéd.

Linda Stone

Camarillo, CA

Catch a Falling Star
32 W x 32 H

Adages and Idioms Challenge
An Elephant in the Room
18 W x 18 H

Lynne Willcox

Simi Valley, CA

This rose fabric reminded me of the paintings of Watteau and Fragonard. The challenge was finding a way to evoke the charming excesses of the French Baroque.

Flowers through the
Mirror of Time
70 W x 21 H

Artists' Walkabout, September 13, 2023

An Extreme Quilters Tradition: The night before gallery opening each artist shares the inspiration and techniques of each piece in the show with the other Extreme Quilters.

Gallery Opening Day
September 14, 2023

Gallery Opening Day
September 14, 2023

Made in the USA
Las Vegas, NV
21 September 2023